Interval

The A.D. Players Series

A Full-length Play
About Relationships

By
Jeannette Clift George
Artistic Director, A.D. Players

Lillenas PUBLISHING COMPANY

KANSAS CITY, MO 64141

The A.D. Players is a Christian theatre company based in Houston, Texas. September 1997 opened their 31st season of production. Their work includes a season of main stage shows at Grace Theater, a season of children's shows in St. Luke's United Methodist Church's Rotunda Theater, a traveling unit, and a program for interns and apprentices. For further information on the company or on this script, contact:

A.D. Players
2710 W. Alabama
Houston, TX 77098

Dedication

Lovingly dedicated to Paul Miller, whose earnest, dedicated work has made it possible for writers like me and programs like yours to enjoy the celebration of Christian drama.

Notes

Interval tells the story of a series of meetings shared by two people over a period of several months. It is set in a corner of Riverside Park, New York City, New York, on Fridays after work, beginning in mid-January.

The two people meet by coincidence, relate by the casual repetition of that meeting, and develop a relationship while discussing the mystery of two murders.

ALAN MITCHELL is a man in his early 30s, recently moved to New York and seeking an answer to deep personal questions.

LENORE BARBER is a young woman in her mid 20s, also newly arrived in New York.

From the conversations between ALAN and LENORE, the details of two mysterious murders are discussed.

Act I, Scene 1—mid-January
Act I, Scene 2—mid-February, Valentine's Day
Act I, Scene 3—some time later
Act I, Scene 4—one week later
Act II, Scene 1—April
Act II, Scene 2—early May
Act II, Scene 3—one week later
Act II, Scene 4—some time later, midweek
Act II, Scene 5—some time later, again on Friday
Act II, Scene 6—one week later

Director's Notes

As you bring this script to life on your stage, you may find several principles helpful to your creative experience. First is the matter of relationship between two characters. As the scenes progress, LENORE and ALAN are to progress into a unique relationship. The scenes chronicle that relationship as specifically as the details of the mystery are told. With each progression the personal relationship becomes more intimate, more accustomed to its happening, and more critical for the reckoning with its signature. The public setting turns into the privacy of home life, and one casual meeting takes on the appearance of a settled marriage with the developing mystery always in the background of each event of meeting. This principle will affect every aspect of the show's production.

The second principle is in LENORE's ability to give ALAN and the audience an in-depth portrayal of all the people she talks about. The actress must detail not only LENORE's character but also every member of the unseen cast. ALAN and the audience must see, recognize, and remember all the people LENORE brings onstage with her. This can be accomplished by becoming the person portrayed in each instance of the dialogue, maintaining a tilt of the head, a gliding of the voice, and a pose of the body. The story requires a full cast brought to our eyes by the work of two people. In order for the plot to unfold, the audience must behold grandmother, grandfather, mother, brother, Mac, Janice, Ramona, and all the personnel LENORE recalls.

Another principle is the reminder that this is a murder mystery. The life statements we see as the story unfolds are of powerful implication, but the sense of a mystery story is never lost. The message is not delivered through a sermon presentation, but through the reality of the people delivering it. The Bible is quoted only as it is part of the generics of the scene, the moral is explored only as it unfolds from real events of real people, and the statement is heard from the choices made in the reality of the story's events.

I hope you enjoy doing this play. It is about two people, drawn together by circumstances, who must confront the validity of faith in the crisis of relationship, and the mystery of two murders. The A.D. Players have offered two successful productions of it, and I think of each one with a longing to do it again. It is wonderful to remember the reaction of audiences who figured out their individual solutions and spent the intermission comparing detective notes. Do keep the mystery a mystery so that each audience can enjoy the delight of surprise contrived just for their entertainment.

Production Notes

Costume Design

Costumes, though contemporary, should be seasonal since the play goes from winter to late summer or even early fall.

Most scenes take place after work, and the clothes would reflect work attire, but since each scene is later than the last, costume changes from scene to scene will be necessary. Most of these have to happen very quickly to avoid lulls between scenes.

We handled this by having a dresser assist each actor and also by creating specially rigged pieces to break away and fasten quickly with Velcro or snaps or other such tricks. Overdressing (wearing one outfit or piece over another) and simply removing it quickly is another technique, but avoid creating an unnatural bulkiness. Coats and scarves in the earlier winter scenes can also be used to hide the following scene's clothes.

For a smooth production it is critical that costume design be thought out in detail and planned very early in the process. Ample rehearsal time must be planned for the actor/dresser teams to be able to learn and execute the changes quickly and smoothly.

Set and Lighting Design

In most murder mysteries, setting and physical placement of objects are important to the plot. *Interval* is no exception.

The setting of this play is a real location in New York City, but rather than go to the expense of traveling there with a Polaroid camera, you can pay close attention to the opening notes of the play. You will find there is much room for creativity while keeping the basic elements of the setting true to the needs of the script. For example, in the opening scene it is important for LENORE to be able to enter, cross to the payphone, and make a call without noticing ALAN sitting on the bench in the area. Careful reading and thought to details will help in arranging the layout of the bench, phone, and so on.

As to style, there can be great creative freedom in suggesting this little, tucked-away corner of a park. But a strong word of caution: trying to be too realistic in foliage, ground cover, bare branches and blooming flowers, real rain and snow to suggest the seasons will quickly accelerate into great costs, manpower, equipment, awkward scene changes, and general mayhem. Our two different productions of this play, designed by different designers, were very different in their look, but both remained very simple. One used a neutral cyclorama background with projected patterns to suggest the trees in their various seasonal attire. Another was more abstract and a little more defined in suggestion of trees, but relied heavily on the color and patterns of lighting to suggest the changing seasons.

The lighting design became crucial to establishing seasons. Each scene takes place after work in the early evening hours. But 5:30 P.M. in winter looks much different than 5:30 P.M. in summer. We used extensive numbers of gobos or patterns in several lights to project shadows of trees and branches in various states of winter bareness, spring budding, and summer shading. Appropriate strong color accents from the top and sides, as well as paler color tints from the front, were mixed with these to suggest a warm or cool atmosphere, depending on the season.

Lighting is also critical in establishing mood. The storm scene in Act I, Scene 3, is not only rainy but also romantic in its intimacy. Attention should be paid to the fact that this is also a murder mystery. Lighting can enhance the feeling of suspense with color, pattern, intensity, direction, and even the intentional use of shadow.

Sound effects of nearby traffic, as well as natural sounds of a park in different seasons, like the rain in Act I, Scene 3, or birds in the spring and summer scenes, can add to realism, but should not be so noticeable as to distract once a scene gets underway. Appropriate but subtle music can both enhance a mood or advance the suspense between scenes.

INTERVAL

Act I

Scene 1

(A park bench, a trash basket, an inoperative drinking fountain, and a public telephone are in the area. A walkway right to left above an embankment leading down to the stage area has steps into the park corner. Downstage and slightly to the right is a railing.

(ALAN MITCHELL is sitting on the bench. It is very cold. He is hunched into the cold. He stands abruptly, waves his arms, and jumps a couple of times, then settles back down on the bench and glances at his watch.

(LENORE BARBER enters up left, very hesitantly. She cannot see ALAN. As she moves into the stage area, she sees the telephone and moves quickly to it. She puts in the coin, waits for the dial tone, and dials.)

LENORE: Hello. May I speak to Janice Leavell, please—if she's still there. *(Pause)* Oh, she is? That's good. *(Pause)* Janice? I was afraid I'd missed you . . . No, that's OK. You said you might have to work late, but I was a little late getting here, and I thought maybe you'd already come by or I was at the wrong place. *(Pause)* No, I'm not under the bridge. I found a telephone in the park. There's a boat dock down there, and I can see walkways and tables and things. I'm only a few feet from the drive. *(Pause)* No, I don't mind waiting here . . . unless you want to stay in town. *(Pause)* I'll see you in a few minutes. *(Checks watch)* Right!

(ALAN has begun his warm-up exercises again. As LENORE hangs up, she sees him and is startled. ALAN sees her looking at him.)

ALAN: Good evening.

LENORE *(very abrupt, dismissing him)*: Good evening.

ALAN: I'm sorry if I frightened you. It's the cold. I have to move around every once in a while. Do you want to sit down?

LENORE: No, thank you. My brothers are coming to meet me here. They're cops. They work this beat . . . and my husband is going to call me in a minute.

ALAN: On the telephone?

LENORE: Yeah.

ALAN: How will he know how to call you?

LENORE: He works for the phone company—part time.

ALAN *(grinning at her obvious fear):* I see. Look, I'm waiting for a ride too. I don't blame you for being scared. You can't be too careful. I'll go. You can sit here and wait. Walking will keep me warm.

LENORE: You don't have to do that. I was just startled to see you jumping around when I didn't know anyone else was here.

ALAN: This isn't a very busy part of the park. I've been coming here for three weeks, and I haven't seen anyone. They don't even pick up the trash. I had a candy bar two weeks ago—there's the wrapper . . . *(Points to trash basket)* just where I left it.

LENORE: You're very neat.

ALAN: Thank you.

LENORE: A lot of people would throw that wrapper on the ground, littering the place. What kind of a place is this?

ALAN: Well, that's the Hudson River. Boat docks are down there. A children's playground is back there. That walkway goes up through the park to Riverside Drive. Out there is the West Side Highway, and the Henry Hudson Parkway is that way.

LENORE: I know. That's where my friend is picking me up.

ALAN: In that little turn-around place?

LENORE: Yeah, we're going to her house in Tarreytown.

ALAN: I hear it's pretty up there.

LENORE: I don't know. I've never seen it. It's an old house where my roommate lived before she moved into the city. We have an apartment in midtown Manhattan.

ALAN: With your brothers and your husband?

LENORE: No, I don't have any of those—any husbands, I mean. I have two sisters. One is married. They live in Wisconsin. I was a little frightened when I first saw you. I've just moved to New York, and everyone has warned me about the horrible things that might happen to me, and when I saw you jumping around like that, I thought sure you were one of those horrible things.

ALAN: I was cold. I'm still cold.

LENORE: I've got some coffee in my Thermos. It may still be hot . . .

ALAN: Don't bother . . .

LENORE: It's no bother. Look, it's still hot. I've an extra cup in the lid, and I think there's a Danish somewhere. . . . Here it is. It's a little mashed, but that won't spoil the taste. *(Empties the sack on the bench)* Do you take cream or sugar?

ALAN: A little sugar, if you have it.

LENORE: Sure.

(LENORE *pours the coffee into the lid and hands it to* ALAN.)

ALAN: Lady, lady, lady. You may have saved my life.

LENORE: Why are you here? You said you came all week?

ALAN: My brother—my *real* brother—picks me up on his way home. He's a floor supervisor at Bloomingdale's. He lives in Englewood. *(Tastes the coffee)* Oh, that's good. I've been in New York since the first of the year. Transferred here from San Francisco.

LENORE: I'm from Wisconsin. Fond-du-Lac.

ALAN: What's the name of it?

LENORE: Fond-du-Lac . . . Wisconsin. It's on Lake Winnebago. It's near Sheboygan. It's a very nice town. I left there three weeks ago. So much has happened in those three weeks. I met my roommate at the agency where I got my job. I'm the receptionist at the Hartley Club on Park Avenue.

ALAN: I haven't been here long enough to know all the clubs.

LENORE *(serving Danish):* This isn't exactly a club. It's a real posh women's residence club—sort of like the Junior League with apartments. It's a good job. My roommate, Janice, got me this job the last day she was working for the agency. Now she works for a chain of boutique shops. You know, high-priced dresses with foreign labels. She travels during the week and was looking for a roommate to take care of her cats and plants, and I was looking for a place to live, and I love cats. . . . I think I've got an apple.

ALAN: No thanks—this is perfect.

(LENORE *takes out napkins.)*

ALAN: What do you keep in your purse—an instant picnic?

LENORE: No. Just a few leftovers. My roommate says I shouldn't take a lunch to work—that's *(imitating roommate)* "small town," but I haven't gotten used to being "big town" yet, and I feel safer knowing what I'll eat—and where. My roommate says I'll miss the "whole experience of New York" because I have lunch with a paper sack. I think you have to work your way up to experiencing New York. You can't do it all at once. First, I experienced the nearest post office; then I experienced a food market near our apartment; then I experienced the bus to work—and that was an experience, believe me. Next week, I'll experience Chock Full O' Nuts. *(Eats apple)*

ALAN: Is New York what you thought it would be?

LENORE: Oh yes. No! Yeah, I guess so. No, not really. It's hard to picture New York when you're in Fond-du-Lac. And each day you're in New York, it's harder to picture Fond-du-Lac. In a way, I was ready for New York. I'd been here when I was a little girl. My grandmother was an actress and lived at the Ansonia. One summer I spent a week with her. It was wonderful. I loved the theatre. My grandmother used to call me the other actress in the family. We went to grand places to eat—places that I never would have seen at home. My grandmother was a beautiful lady—very tall and slender. She had a habit of arching her neck like a swan, and she looked at everybody as though they had just paid her a compliment. I loved being here. Grandmother wasn't working, and we had time to be together. She said *(Begins the style of her narration, which is to take on the vocal and body signature she is quoting. She continues this style throughout the play.)*, "It's the perfect week for you to be here. I'm between plays and have time to be your grandmother. When one is being an actress in a play, one has not time to be anything else." I loved the way she said "actress."

ALAN: She was not American?

LENORE: Yes, but she spoke with an accent. No one ever knew why. She had never been anywhere that people spoke as she did. If you asked her about it, she said, "I speak the language of my heart. The accent is in your ear. I'm afraid it is foreign." The first time I heard her say that, I cupped my hands over my ears. My mother thought I was being rude and slapped my hands away. I cried and said, "I just wanted to know what 'foreign' feels like." My mother didn't understand, just shook her head. My grandfather understood. He picked me up and hugged me real close. *(Closes her eyes, remembering the closeness of the moment)* He had a short blunt beard that was scratchy, and he smelled of working in the sun. He was always kind. He was very, very wise. "You can't feel what's foreign," he said, "because when you're in touch with the 'foreign,' you find it as friendly as your own ear." Mother said, "Papa! You'll spoil that child with your nonsense. You'd like to baby her forever." And then my grandmother said, "Clarence, what's to become of us? We have a daughter who was never a child and a granddaughter who may never grow up. We must have done something dreadfully wrong." And then they looked at each other and laughed—a secret kind of laugh they always shared. It was like a curtain that closed out the world. They were a strange couple. She was tall and very beautiful. He was short and plain. When he sat down, he crossed his legs at the ankle because they were too short to cross at the knee. He was from New England, a farmer.

ALAN: How did they get together?

LENORE: They met when she was playing summer stock in New Hampshire . . . were married in a chapel in Boston on a Sunday night after a performance. She was still in her stage makeup, and when he raised her veil to kiss her, she was crying mascara tears.

ALAN: That's very romantic. Fond-du-Lac, Wisconsin, is a very prosaic choice for so romantic a couple.

LENORE: She didn't choose it. He did. They were visiting in Fond-du-Lac, and he said to her, "Mae, you're going to travel all over the world, but this is where you'll live. I hope you like it." So they bought a farm and built a big, gray house and raised a family. When their children were grown, she went back into theatre.

ALAN: Did he stay in Fond-du-Lac?

LENORE: He always went to see her shows, wherever they were, and then they'd come back together to the big, gray farmhouse in Fond-du-Lac. Her apartment in New York was a lot more fun than the big, gray house. When you entered the front door, you were in the kitchen! A little, tiny kitchen. And then there was a long room with chairs and a pale, pink sofa that had purple, fringed tassels that touched the floor. *(Walks it out as she remembers it)* On the other side of the bookshelf room divider was a great, big, oval bed with pillows of all sizes and colors. And everything smelled purple. And we would get sandwiches from a delicatessen, and I'd sit on her pink sofa, and she would read plays to me.

ALAN: Was she a famous actress?

LENORE: She was a good actress—everybody said. She played in a lot of theatres and traveled with what they called industrial shows. Then one spring, I was 11—or was I 12?—my braces were off—must have been 12—I don't remember—she was cast in a big show written by Tennessee Williams. She had a wonderful role, and we all planned to go to New York to see the Broadway opening. *Life* magazine did an article on the play, and my grandmother was in all the pictures. The papers in Fond-du-Lac were filled with news of her and the play.

ALAN: That's famous. I've never known anyone whose grandmother made *Life* magazine. Was the play a hit?

LENORE: Not when it opened in Boston. It didn't get good reviews. They called in a play doctor who wrote my grandmother out of the play.

ALAN: That's a shame. Was she very disappointed?

LENORE: Oh, yes. It was to have been her big break. She would have been a star on Broadway.

ALAN: What did she do?

LENORE: She came home.

ALAN: You mean she gave up her career?

LENORE: It was very strange. Grandfather called us and said they were coming home, and no one was to say anything to her until she spoke to them. I remember the day they arrived. My father picked them up at the train station. My sisters and I watched them drive up to the house. We were hiding behind the curtains in the dining room window. My father and my grandfather helped my grandmother out of the car as though she were very old or had been very ill. She had on a black dress with a ruffle and wore a hat with a dark veil. Grandfather helped her into the house and up the stairs to their room. No one said a word—not one word. There she stayed for four days. She never came out. Only my grandfather went into her room, carrying trays of crackers and soup. All the time she was in there, we heard her sobbing and crying. It was awful. My mother and grandfather would argue about my grandmother making such a fuss locked up in her room. Mother said, "Well, *someone* has to do *something*. She'll die up there. Raymond," that's my father, who was away on a business trip, "Raymond says he's not coming back until she's out of that room!" One day, I was standing by the stairs listening to Grandmother moaning. Mother was in the dining room with Grandfather. She said, "It's not good for the children to hear all that carrying on. I'm going up there. I'm going in that room and tell her to control herself!" My grandfather was very stern. "Leave her alone, Jettie. She knows what she's doing." Then he saw me. I was scared. It's scary for kids when adults argue. Don't you think so?

ALAN: Yes. The kids don't understand. Little ones expect big ones to have all their problems worked out.

LENORE: Exactly.

ALAN: Tell me the rest of the story. What did your grandfather do when he saw you?

LENORE: He came over to me and took my hand. Then he led me out to the front yard. We had a big, old tree with a bench around it. He sat me there and talked to me as though I were as wise as he. And I listened smarter than I'd ever heard before. "We're going to talk about your grandmother. It's nothing to be scared about. Your grandmother is grieving out a great hurt. We'll help her by waiting for her to finish with it. Some folk here don't understand. You and I know that what she's doing isn't strange—it's perfectly reasonable. Your grandmother is a reasonable woman. We must be reasonable with her grieving—and wait. She's going to be all right. We know that—you and I. She'll come out of that room prettier and sweeter and stronger than she's ever been. Do you know why?" I shook my head—scarcely breathing. Being treated like an adult can be suffocating. "When she comes out to us, she will have learned she can outlive her dreams. When you know that, and know that you know that, you can live all your life—and you're *strong*." (ALAN *moves away.*) Well, it happened just like he said. One morning, real early, Grandmother came out of that room wearing a pink, flowery dress. Her eyes were clear, her nose wasn't red. She didn't even have a Kleenex in her hand. She looked prettier and younger than we'd ever seen her. She smiled at everybody and went into the kitchen and made a batch of pecan snaffles—just like nothing had happened.

ALAN: What did your grandfather say?

LENORE: Nothing. Nobody did. Nobody ever mentioned it to her, and she never mentioned it to us. She never did a play again, never even talked about theatre. I don't know what happened to her apartment here because she stayed in the big, gray house in Fond-du-Lac until the day she died.

ALAN: No, I mean what did he say to you out under the tree?

LENORE: Oh, he said I was to tell my sisters not to laugh at her or ask any questions.

ALAN: No—what did he say about dreams?

LENORE: That she would outlive them—and that that was good. I don't know what of that I understood then, but it makes sense now.

(ALAN *and* LENORE *sit in silence for a moment, having shared a great thought.*)

LENORE: Oh my goodness! I don't think I have ever talked this much in my whole life. (*Begins gathering coffee cups, Thermos, and so on*) I'm sorry. I guess I haven't had anyone to talk to since I've been here. I don't know the people where I work, and my roommate is gone all the time—my roommate! Oh, good grief! I better get out there. I hope I haven't made you miss your ride.

ALAN: No, my brother always works late. He'll be another 30 minutes yet. I'll throw that away. . . . You better hurry to catch your ride.

LENORE: Yes, I will. Thank you. Good-bye. Oh, in case we meet again, I'm Lenore.

ALAN: I'm Alan. Have a nice weekend.

LENORE: I will. You too. Good-bye.

(LENORE *runs up and off left.* ALAN *stands watching her. He tosses napkins in the trash, walks to rail, shudders, and is suddenly very cold.*)

(*Lights*)

Scene 2

(*One month later. The trash basket is gone.* LENORE *enters, looks around for* ALAN. *She moves to bench, puts down a New York shopping bag, opens it, takes out a couple of small sacks, and places them on the bench. She looks around again for* ALAN. *She goes to the telephone, drops in coin, and dials.*)

LENORE: Hello, this is Lenore. Is Janice near the phone? . . . You don't need to get her; you could give her a message. (*Pause*) Hi, Janice, it's me, Lenore. I tried to tell him not to bother you. I'm here. (*Pause*) About 30 minutes? OK. Hey, you got a package at the apartment. It was delivered yesterday. I left it there. I didn't know if you might be in the apartment today. (*Pause*) Sure, it wouldn't take you more than five minutes to pick it up . . . OK. See you.

(LENORE *sees* ALAN *entering from down right carrying the empty trash basket.*)

LENORE: Hi. I thought you weren't here.

ALAN: I took out the trash.

LENORE *(laughing):* It was already out! Where did you take it?

ALAN: I dumped it in an empty one up by 86th. I don't think anyone comes here. Everything was right where we'd left it—all the way down to that first candy bar wrapper. Each day's newspaper stacked on top.

LENORE: We could write a note of protest to the park commissioner. Wait . . . turn it upside down. We can use it for a table.

ALAN: What have you got there?

LENORE: The remains of a Valentine party. A debutante luncheon at the club. We got the leftovers. We got mints and little cakes. I can't tell the decorations from the refreshments, so I brought a little of everything. *(Empties a dress box and places it on upturned trash basket)* Help yourself. *(Setting "table")* Happy Valentine's Day.

ALAN: No, thank you.

LENORE: You have a party at your office?

ALAN: No, I don't eat a lot of sweets. I'll have some of the nuts though. Cashews? My favorites.

LENORE: And—I brought you a present.

(LENORE hands ALAN what was in the dress box.)

ALAN: Why?

LENORE: Because it's Valentine's, and it's something you need, and the doorman at the club was selling them. His wife makes them. His name is Mac Forrestor. He's a Scot. He speaks with such a heavy accent I never know what he's saying—but he's very nice. He's always selling something. *(With thick Scottish burr)* "Here you are, Miss Barber, I saved one just for you."

ALAN: What is it?

LENORE: Foot warmers. Loafer socks. You always sit here complaining that your feet are cold.

ALAN: That was just because of the snow.

LENORE: And you wouldn't wear overshoes. See if they fit. Mac said one size fits all. Do they fit?

ALAN: One of them does. They're warm too. Feels good.

LENORE: Then have some coffee and tell me about your day.

ALAN: What do you mean?

LENORE: What happened in your day? What did you do?

ALAN: I went to work.

LENORE: But that's not what happened. Tell me what you did.

ALAN: I worked.

LENORE: At what?

ALAN: I've told you. I'm an account executive. I execute accounts.

LENORE: Yes, at Walton's Import and Export. That sounds exciting.

ALAN: Why?

LENORE: Imports and exports. Comings and goings. Isn't that exciting?

ALAN: Not when you're an account executive. You just do a lot of paperwork.

LENORE: Then that's what you do! You work with papers.

ALAN: No, I work with accounts. That's why I'm an . . .

LENORE and ALAN *(in unison):* . . . account executive. *(They laugh.)*

LENORE: I know that. You told me all that last week. You were transferred here . . .

ALAN: To a better job.

LENORE: To a better job. You live with your brother in Englewood who picks you up here each Friday.

ALAN: Right.

LENORE: But what do you do? At work, what do you do?

ALAN: Well, today I nearly went crazy trying to locate 350 Italian music boxes. They should have been here 10 days ago, and I've got an angry client who is about to cancel his order.

LENORE: What'll you do if he does?

ALAN: If he cancels? I'll start praying that those 350 Italian music boxes never get here. If they do, *I'll* have to peddle them.

LENORE: That's terrible.

ALAN: You're telling me. But I think they're here. I just feel it in my bones. Those music boxes are in a shipment that's here. They've got the wrong labels, but they're here. Monday I'll go down to the docks myself, prowl around all those crates, and pray those 350 music boxes get turned on! Can't you imagine— the docks at dawn, and all of a sudden 350 music boxes!

(ALAN begins to hum Italian tunes. LENORE joins in. They laugh at the thought.)

LENORE: That's funny.

ALAN: It's good to laugh about it. Not much else I can do until Monday.

LENORE: You said you'd be doing all that praying. You say that a lot. Do you mean any of it?

ALAN: What?

LENORE: Praying. Are you that kind of person, the praying kind?

ALAN: Yeah.

LENORE: I wish I believed in that. It would change my life.

ALAN: Yeah, it would.

LENORE: I don't go to church. I don't believe in it. I don't think you should go to church unless you believe in it. It's better than a bar for meeting people, and it's a good answer for loneliness, but that's deceitful. I mean—you don't go to a grocery store to improve your social life, why go to a church to make dates? That's stupid, and I refuse to do it.

ALAN: Hey, hey. Why pick on me? All I did was tell you I believe in prayer.

LENORE: I know . . . and I don't.

(Pause)

ALAN: So I see. I do believe in God. I believe that He did that most amazing thing—became man, flesh and blood. I believe in that Christ. Sometimes I am angered by what He does in my life. I don't have the easy answers I used to have. But I know that God loves. Somewhere in all the pain is the love of God.

LENORE: But do you really believe He is involved—like a person—in your life?

ALAN: He's involved all right.

LENORE: If God were right here, I mean standing right here, what would you ask Him for?

ALAN: Forgiveness—and to make all the ugliness never have happened.

LENORE: Do you believe He could do that if He were standing right here?

ALAN: I believe He is here. I'm not sure what He's going to do.

LENORE: If He finds your 300 music boxes, I'll look into a church.

ALAN: It's 350, and who started all this talk about church?

LENORE: My mother and a bunch of cousins who are not much for church themselves but would feel better about me if I were in a church. I guess they figure I can get along on my own in Fond-du-Lac, but I need a lot of help in New

York. My roommate says I am "haunted by the echoes of a conservative background." She's really nice. She gave me this coat. Look—it's got a zip-out lining. We wear the same size. This is one she had and never wore. She's trying to teach me style. I like going to her place on weekends. We fix supper in this big kitchen, and then we light a fire and sit and talk. She tells me about the newest fashions, and I tell her all the things happening at the office. She likes to hear about the people there. They are characters. Mr. Slocum—that's the boss—he's a tall, good-lookin' man, mid-40s, very successful, very intense. He moves fast; he talks fast, like one of those wind-up toys that goes to the edge of the table and then turns around. "Call Mr. Abercrombie and tell him I'll meet him in Philadelphia on the 20th. You get that?" He has an office you wouldn't believe. It's half of the second floor, and it's gorgeous. He's got a new secretary who goes well with the furnishings. Her name is Ramona, and she kind of yawns when she talks. "Ra-moan-a." The talk is that when Mrs. Slocum sees Ramona, Mr. Slocum will get a new secretary. I've only seen Mrs. Slocum once. They live in White Plains, and she comes in to the city once a week to get her hair done. I was at my desk last week when I heard Mr. Slocum say, "Estelle, come meet our new receptionist, Lenore Barber." I got up and came around my desk and saw this lovely, blond lady bending down talking to old Mrs. Whyler. She's lived at the Hartley longer than anybody. I put out my hand and said, "Mrs. Slocum," and when she turned around, I saw the blankest blue eyes I've ever seen, like someone who had practiced not seeing anything. She smiled *through* me and said, "Mr. Slocum tells me what a wonderful work you're doing. Are you enjoying being in New York?" I told her that I was, and before I could say anything else, Mr. Slocum had her out the door, and Mac was putting her in her car. I think there's something wrong there. He usually stays in town except weekends. Maybe she's ill or they're having trouble. Mr. Slocum seems like a nice man. He works hard, stays late. He always waves when he passes my desk. This morning he was waiting at the elevator when I came in. "Good morning, Lenore." He always remembers everyone's name. "You look like you're wearing a rainbow. I hope it'll bring out the sun."

ALAN: Why didn't you go into theatre like your grandmother? You act out everyone you know.

LENORE: I wanted to be an actress for a while. Then I was in the senior play in high school. I was pretty bad. My mother said I was the prettiest one in it, and my father said I had certainly learned my lines well. It was my grandfather who talked to me about theatre as a career. I was watching him paint a new chicken coop, and I asked him what he thought about my "talent." "Should I go into theatre?" "Well," he said, painting real carefully along an edge, "it all depends on you. If you need theatre bad enough, you can spend your life convincing it that it needs you. Or you can adjust to the fact that theatre doesn't need you and be just as happy doing something else." I didn't really mind. All I wanted out of theatre was an apartment at the Ansonia like my grandmother had.

ALAN: Is your grandfather still living?

LENORE: Oh, yeah. Sure. They're all alive and well back in Fond-du-Lac, except my grandmother. My grandfather's a Christian. He's got a Bible, and he goes to a little church near the farm. He can't get anyone to go with him though. About a year ago he stopped asking us.

ALAN: He's a wise man, in many ways.

LENORE *(looking at watch):* Well, I'll put these things away. You could probably leave those slippers here. No one would disturb them. I'll put the box top behind the bench, in case we need it again.

ALAN: I'll put all that up. Go on, don't miss your ride.

LENORE: OK. Have a nice weekend.

ALAN: Sure. Thanks for the slippers.

LENORE: Sure. Bye. Oh, Happy Valentine's.

ALAN: Yeah. Thanks.

(Lights)

Scene 3

(Trash basket is missing. ALAN's briefcase is propped against bench. LENORE enters, carrying a sack as in the previous scene. She places the sack by the up corner of the bench and systematically goes to work setting up the area. From the bushes, she lifts a radio, sets it on the fountain, and dials to music. From behind the bench, she lifts out slippers and places them on the ground in front of the bench. From area behind the telephone, she gets a canvas chair, sets it up at the lower corner of the bench, and stands and looks for ALAN in the distance. She unpacks items in the sack and stacks them on the up right section of the bench. Again she looks for ALAN. She opens one sack to lift out sandwiches and chips. She goes to the telephone, drops in coins, and dials.)

LENORE: Hi. This is Lenore. Tell Janice I called and . . . no, I don't want to talk to her. Just tell her I called. *(Pause)* Yeah, it looks like we're in for more rain. Well, I guess she could call me here. This number is 555-4891. It's a public phone.

(ALAN enters carrying the trash basket.)

LENORE: I'll wait here until she calls. *(Hangs up phone)*

ALAN: I took out the trash. Way out. The 86th Street cage was bashed flat. Finally found one at 93rd.

LENORE: Oh well, another letter to the park commissioner.

(ALAN *leaves basket in place, overturned.* LENORE *slides a tray from under the bench.* ALAN *changes to slippers and unfolds newspaper while* LENORE *prepares the table: paper plates and napkins set, candles in holders, coffee poured, and artificial flowers placed.*)

LENORE: I called Janice and left this number for her to call back. She has a client in the showroom. I hope she gets back before the rain. I left my raincoat when I went home for lunch.

ALAN: Talked to my brother. He might be able to leave a little early. Severe storm warnings. Oh, I brought you a present.

(ALAN *hands* LENORE *a package wrapped in newspaper. She is affected by his first gift to her.*)

LENORE: What's the occasion?

ALAN: You'll see.

LENORE: A music box! An Italian music box!

ALAN: Three hundred forty-nine to go. They came in today. Went to Spain.

LENORE: Why?

ALAN: It's the height of the tourist season. All Italy goes to Spain. How should I know? They got mixed up someplace. But they're all here now.

LENORE: Is your client pleased? (*Begins playing the music box*)

ALAN: What client? He canceled. I told you that. No client's going to wait around for some bungling account executive to find his music boxes in Spain.

LENORE: You didn't bungle it. The shippers did.

ALAN: They know I'm a novice and they can get by with it.

LENORE: That's ridiculous. How could they know you're just beginning?

ALAN: How can they know? Somebody tells them. That's how they know. Let me tell you something. All the world is alerted to the weak link: the newest clerk, the incompetent salesman, the poor kid who's never learned the language, the littlest little leaguer. What are the sandwiches?

LENORE: Chicken salad. I made them myself.

ALAN: Had that for lunch.

LENORE: I've got some cookies and half a cheese Danish.

ALAN: Any fruit?

LENORE: Yeah. I've got an orange, some grapes, an apple . . .

ALAN: A banana—got a banana?

LENORE: No.

ALAN: Any nuts?

LENORE: The cashews! *(Goes to bushes)* They might be a little stale, but we sealed the can with scotch tape and put it in this coffee can. How are they?

ALAN: They'll be OK.

LENORE: Thanks for the music box. I like them. Such a gentle sound. I'll be glad to endorse your product if it'll help your sales. *(Pause)* Everyone at the club is going off in all directions. A big wedding tonight. One of the biggest they've ever had. We've got two extra doormen. Mac is calling out directions to them, and they don't understand one word he says. The florists came in this morning. A bank of orchids flown in! A bank covering one whole wall of the ballroom! Can you imagine what they cost? We've got people coming in and out those doors like ants—special caterers, special designers, an extension to the canopy. How are the nuts?

ALAN: OK. A little stale.

LENORE: We've got a young girl working part-time. Trish is like a coffee girl for the executive staff. All she has done today is gawk at everything and everybody. I was typing the guest list for security, and she came running in shouting, "Miz Barber, Miz Barber! Two movie stars just came in for lunch. Two of them. I've never seen two of them at once before in my life." "Who are they?" I said. "One of them is Debbie Reynolds, and the other is that actress who exercises and hates war. I can't remember her name, but I'll get her autograph." I told her Mr. Slocum advises the staff to refrain from that. "He can't refrain me. He owes my daddy a favor. That's why I got this job. All I have to do is show up!" *(Telephone rings)* I'll get it. That's Janice. Hello. *(Pause)* Oh, OK. Let's try it. *(To ALAN)* Janice called in from the showroom. They're going to try to patch us together. Janice has a real bad cold. She shouldn't have gone to work today but . . . yeah, I'm here. Hello. Hello? No, I can't hear anybody. Maybe it won't work with a public phone. *(Pause)* Well, Les, just tell her I'll be at the usual spot in . . . how long? OK. Twenty minutes. I'll be standing under the bridge if it's raining.

ALAN: It'll be raining. No doubt about that. It's starting to sprinkle.

(ALAN *reaches behind the bench and gets two umbrellas.* LENORE *joins him, each sitting feet up on the bench covered by umbrellas. We hear thunder, and the lights darken as the storm moves in.* LENORE *grabs two candles, hands one to* ALAN *and holds the other. The personal intimacy of their relationship is reflected in the scene.)*

LENORE: Is this an illustration of rain on the just and the unjust?

ALAN: It may be. I wonder which is which?

LENORE: You're the just, and I'm the unjust.

28

ALAN: Why?

LENORE: You're the churched, and I'm the unchurched.

ALAN: For someone not interested in religion, you harp on it an awful lot.

LENORE: I'm fascinated by your deep faith.

ALAN: Because I believe in God? That's not deep. That's just touching the surface. You've got a deeper faith than I have.

LENORE *(laughing):* I don't have any faith at all.

ALAN: Oh, yes, you do! You have a resolute faith in God's insignificance. You are determined to believe He doesn't exist.

LENORE: No, I believe He exists. Somehow, in some form. I believe there is a force, a power, that exists. I don't believe it's a "he" or a "she." I've never been interested in religions. No, really, I haven't. Maybe I should be. Maybe I'm a latent Hindu or a Moonie. I'm probably a Universalist.

ALAN: What's that?

LENORE: A Universalist? You don't know what a Universalist is?

ALAN: I don't know what you are that may be a Universalist.

LENORE: Well, I don't know what a Universalist is either. But I may be one.

ALAN: Last night my brother was trying to explain God to his little boy, Budgie.

LENORE: The one who hid the frog in the Cuisinart?

ALAN: Yeah. Budgie asked if God had a mommy. Carl stammered a while and tried to come up with some suitable answer. He teaches a Bible class for college seniors. He talked about God being self-created, preexistent. Budgie just stared at him. Finally, *I* asked Budgie why he wanted to know if God had a mommy. He said he wondered who got God up every morning.

LENORE: What did you tell him?

ALAN: I told him that God got up the morning, and the moon and the stars and the sun. Budgie was sitting in his dad's lap. All that theology was making him sleepy. But he said, "If He's up before all of them, He must be awfully tired all the time." Then Carl told him about Isaiah 40.

LENORE: What in the world is Isaiah 40?

ALAN: It's in the Bible.

LENORE: What does it say?

ALAN: "Don't you know? Hasn't anyone told you that the Everlasting God, the Lord, the Creator of the ends of the earth never gets weary or tired? His understanding is beyond our understanding. He gives strength to the weary, and to the powerless He gives His might. When little boys get sleepy and tired, and young men—young men—stumble badly . . ." *(Stopping suddenly)*

LENORE *(pause, then supplies continuing verse):* "Yet those who wait for the Lord will renew their strength. They will mount up with wings like eagles. They will run and not be tired, they will walk and not become weary."

(Pause)

ALAN: Where did you learn that?

LENORE: My grandfather. I didn't know I knew it. Did Budgie have any more questions?

ALAN: No. He fell asleep, but he'll remember that time.

LENORE: I'd better get going. Janice will be along in a minute.

ALAN: I'll put everything up. Take an umbrella. It's a bad night.

LENORE: I should take this one back anyway. I think it's Mrs. Slocum's. She was in such a state when she came by she forgot everything. I don't think she likes Ramona. No wife would. Oh, a funny thing happened yesterday. It made us all uncomfortable.

ALAN: You can tell me next week. Hurry. You'll be late.

LENORE: OK. Bye.

(ALAN goes to the telephone, inserts his coins, and dials.)

ALAN: Mr. Carl Mitchell, please. Oh? Is he still on the floor? Tell him his brother called. I'm going to stay in town this weekend. Be sure to tell him. I'll see him Monday. Thanks.

(Lights)

Scene 4

(ALAN sits reading the paper. The basket is ready for table service but with no trimmings. LENORE enters upstage left, above usual entrance.)

LENORE: Hi, Alan. I'm sorry I'm late. We all had to work late. Have you heard what happened?

ALAN: Yeah. I didn't know it was your office until Tuesday.

LENORE: The whole club is swarming with reporters and detectives. I don't like it. Everyone in the office is scared to death. We think it had to be someone who works in the building. All of a sudden everyone has a motive—even the flighty little coffee girl, Trish. We're learning that her father would have had

Mr. Slocum's job, but there was some wheeling and dealing in the management. It's awful being there and suspecting everyone. I can't stay. Janice is in Atlanta for the weekend, and I'm staying in town. I have a taxi waiting. I wanted to bring you some coffee.

ALAN: That's OK. I don't need it. Are you sure you're all right?

LENORE: No, I'm not. But I guess I really am. I've never been around a murder before. It's not like what you see in the movies or the television. Everything is awful and takes forever. I've not been in his office. I don't want to see it. Ramona says it's been chalked where they found Mr. Slocum's body. Whoever murdered him planned it well. They knew so many details about security. And I feel like . . . Oh, never mind. I'll see you next week—if nothing else happens. *(Jumps up and looks over her shoulder as though seeing someone)* Hello? Who is that? Who is there?

ALAN: Is someone coming? *(Moves to ramp)*

LENORE: No. It's just me. I keep thinking I'm being followed. Would you mind walking me to the taxi?

ALAN: Sure. Here, let me get my things, and I'll leave with you.

(ALAN returns to the bench. LENORE exits as ALAN straightens the basket, replaces the tray, and gets his paper and briefcase. The bushes at center move as if a figure would pass.)

ALAN: Yeah. You forget something? Lenore?

(We hear footsteps and see something of a presence moving off right.)

LENORE *(entering left)*: Hurry. I told the cab we're coming.

(ALAN looks off right.)

LENORE: What are you waiting for?

ALAN: Strange. I've never seen anyone in this part of the park before. *(Exit)*

(Lights)

Act II

Scene 1

(The season has changed, but not the set. It is April. The table is set up as before but without the candles. The radio is on. ALAN is not wearing his slippers. A sack is by his briefcase. LENORE is picking wildflowers for a small vase she will add to the center of the table.)

LENORE: I can't believe how slow detectives are. They have questioned everyone over and over again. The secretaries in the pool can't get any work done. Our whole bookkeeping system has been shut down until the new manager gets here. I would like to quit, but no one dares to leave because that would look suspicious.

ALAN: Do the police have leads?

LENORE: Not that they share with us. They let us back in Mr. Slocum's office after dusting everything for fingerprints. Of course, ours were all over everything.

ALAN: Do all of you work in and out of his office?

LENORE: At some time. Trish, the coffee girl, runs errands from that office to the kitchen or the secretary's office or our reception desk. I was up there the day of the murder because Mr. Slocum wanted a copy of the guest list, and I called the photographer from Mr. Slocum's phone. Any of us could have done it. Ramona is hysterical. She knows the police suspect her. Mac, the doorman, has had a total personality change. He never smiles. He grumbles at all of us and has been looking at me as though he'd never even seen me before.

ALAN: Do they think robbery was the motive?

LENORE: No. Nothing was missing except Mr. Slocum's keys.

ALAN: His keys are missing?

LENORE: Yeah. Isn't that strange? One of the detectives figured that out. His name is Bruce Presley, and he can ask more questions than your nephew. He knows everything about me except this.

ALAN: This? You mean bananas and cashews? He's never heard of bananas and cashews? Well, don't fault him for that. They don't cover special things like that in detective school.

LENORE: He got a degree in criminology at the University of Washington and will be studying in England for his master's. He wants to teach at a university in the Midwest and was on the police force in Portland for two years. His hobby is building miniature boats that really sail.

32

ALAN: Hmmm. He seems to have answered a few questions himself. Why didn't he find out about the bananas and cashews?

LENORE: I've not told anyone about this. I don't know why! It's been a kind of special place. I feel safe here. It's the only place in New York where I feel I *belong*. I didn't want to talk about it to outsiders.

ALAN: Maybe we're the outsiders. Maybe the world has excluded us.

LENORE: Well, it included me when Mr. Slocum got himself murdered. I stand at my desk and look up into his office area and can't believe what's happened.

ALAN: How can you see his office? Isn't it on the second floor?

LENORE: Yeah. It's really a half floor up. *(Walks out the area to show him)* You see, the front door is here. The reception desk, that's me, is here. The switchboard is here, the cloak room is here, and the main ballroom is here. Then there are elevators back here, and a big, sweeping stairway is here curving up to the second floor. The secretaries are here, and the manager's office suite is here. Ramona sits here and . . .

ALAN: Are these doors locked?

LENORE: Oh, yes. When everyone leaves, Mac locks all the offices. The residents get to their apartments by the elevator. Mr. Slocum always worked late. If Ramona left before he finished, he would drop his dictation in a little slot in this door and take the stairs down. In the mornings, he usually took the elevator. Why did you ask?

ALAN: I just wondered which keys were missing.

LENORE: I don't know. Bruce noticed there were no keys on . . . on the . . . body and began to inquire if it was Mr. Slocum's custom to carry keys. Since then, they have his house under protection of some kind, thinking Mr. Slocum may have been killed to get the keys to the house.

ALAN: How is Mrs. Slocum?

LENORE: Well, she was hospitalized for shock. I saw her at the funeral, and she looked awful. Probably heavily sedated. She never looked at any one of us. As she was being led back to her car, she suddenly jerked away and ran over to Mr. Slocum's sister who was standing by the casket. Everybody was so startled we just stood and stared while Mrs. Slocum cried out, "I'm sorry, Glenda. I'm so sorry." When she did that, everyone who suspected her looked smug and nodded. I don't think she did it.

ALAN: Why not?

LENORE: Why kill someone at the office you can just as easily kill in your own kitchen? Besides, she hated coming into town. But she did have a motive: Ramona. I think the "business" of that relationship had changed.

ALAN: You've never liked Ramona.

LENORE: I don't trust blonds. They never wrinkle their brows when they worry.

ALAN *(laughing)*: What?

LENORE: They never wrinkle their brows. Haven't you noticed that? Blonds—real blonds—are always smooth from here up. They just stare at the rest of us while we wrinkle and furrow.

ALAN: Maybe blonds don't have anything to worry about. Have you ever thought of that?

LENORE: Cute, real cute. Here I am trying to solve a murder, and you're doing Neil Simon.

ALAN: OK. Let's solve the murder. Whom do we have as suspects?

LENORE: Everyone in the whole world because anyone could have gotten in the building and waited until the five o'clock exodus. Because of the wedding, nobody kept a good watch on the door. However, the murderer knew about the wedding, knew where Mr. Slocum's office was, and was someone Mr. Slocum knew.

ALAN: How come?

LENORE: Mr. Slocum opened his door to him—or to her—or to them. Mac had not locked the outside door to Ramona's office, but Ramona always locked the inside office door when she left, which, by the way, was very unusual. She usually stayed until Mr. Slocum left, but that week she had been leaving early. We think they met somewhere.

ALAN: Did they find the gun?

LENORE: No. It was not there when Paul, that's the security guard, found the body.

ALAN: How about him? Is he a suspect?

LENORE: Who?

ALAN: Paul. The security guard.

LENORE: Oh, no. There's no connection there at all. He only works part-time. He covers the front door until the night doorman comes on at 8:00. He has another job at a bank and relieves Mac at 6:00. The murder was before 6:00. The coroner established that. He's not a suspect.

ALAN: So, we have Ramona—the beautiful blond, Mrs. Slocum—the long-suffering wife, Trish and her revengeful dad . . .

LENORE: That's right. Don't forget them. And one other.

ALAN: Who? Someone you forgot to mention?

LENORE: No, I mentioned him. Mac.

ALAN: The doorman?

LENORE: Uh-huh!

ALAN: Why?

LENORE: Well, he's the kind of man who always has a deal going, and because of the way he's been acting since the murder. He asked me to have lunch with him today, not in the coffee room where we eat the leftovers from the fancy dinners but at, as he said, "a wee little place down the street where we might talk. I think we have something interesting to discuss." I didn't go, but he said, "Then we'll set it for later." It gives me the shivers.

ALAN: Don't go with him. Stay away from him.

LENORE: Why?

ALAN: Because you might get hurt or get involved in someone else's hurt.

(There is a pause as LENORE *hears* ALAN'*s concern for her.)*

LENORE *(close to tears):* Thank you for caring.

ALAN *(hand out to her):* Lenore, I want to tell you something.

LENORE: Oh dear!

ALAN: It's not about the murder. It's something more personal than that. I want to tell you that . . .

LENORE: No, please don't. Not now.

ALAN: Do you know what I'm going to say?

LENORE: I think I do, and I don't want to hear it now.

ALAN: Why not?

LENORE: Because it's time for my ride, and I want to be able to talk about it when you tell me.

ALAN: But I really want . . .

LENORE: Please. Please.

ALAN: OK, you run on. I'll put these things away. Leave the radio. I'll catch the six o'clock news.

LENORE: Thank you. Bye. *(Turns suddenly and hugs him)* Thank you.

(LENORE *exits.* ALAN *stands a moment and then begins to remove the tabletop, glances at his watch, moves to the radio, and changes the station. Deep in thought, he moves to the rail and gazes out front as he hears the radio. At the announcement, he turns slowly full back to stare at the radio.)*

ANNOUNCER: Good evening. This is Peter Ralson with the six o'clock news. A late bulletin reports another death at Park Avenue's exclusive private residence club The Hartley. The body was discovered in the office of the recently slain club manager and has been identified as Mac Forrestor, Hartley Club doorman. The father of a part-time worker at the club entered the office seeking his daughter . . .

(Lights)

Scene 2

(Early May. LENORE *enters. She's dressed up. She sets up the radio, starts to set up the table, realizes the trash basket is as left last visit with a newspaper and the leftovers from the last meeting. She empties the sack she is carrying, tosses the trash in it, sets up the table and waits. She glances at her watch. No* ALAN. *Slowly, she guesses he is not coming and begins to cry as the lights fade.)*

(Lights)

Scene 3

(One week later. The trash basket is empty. ALAN *is seated reading the paper.* LENORE *enters as usual.)*

LENORE: Hello, Alan. Here, you can set up the table while I call Janice.

ALAN: You don't need to put out all that stuff. I'm not hungry.

LENORE: I don't mind. I didn't bring much. We're not having a lot of parties at the club. You know about Mac, the doorman?

*(*LENORE *goes to the telephone, inserts coins, and dials.)*

ALAN: Yeah. I'm sorry.

LENORE: I am too. I feel guilty because I suspected him. Hi. Is Janice still there? *(To* ALAN*)* I worked a little late filling in for the secretaries. The new manager is here. *(To phone)* Janice, it's me. I had to work late. Oh, how long will you be? *(Pause)* No, I'll be OK. I've got my radio and a lot of people are out in the park . . . OK. I'll see you then. *(To* ALAN*)* Janice wants me to quit. She says it's not safe there. She's looking at another apartment. What do you mean "stuff"? I think it's nice to have these things. I didn't bring much except coffee. Last week I had a cake. They had a reception for an author from England. You missed a choice dessert: chocolate ribbon cake.

ALAN: I wasn't in town.

LENORE: Why would you call it "all that stuff"? I try to fix something special each time.

ALAN: I don't want anything.

LENORE: OK. You don't have to eat anything.

ALAN: What's that?

LENORE: They call it French Lace. It's chocolate. Break off a piece. You'll like it.

ALAN: How are people taking this second murder?

LENORE: We're all in shock. Trish's father found Mac's body, you know. He couldn't find Trish and was frantic. Turned out she was at school rehearsing some kind of honors program. Have some more candy. I've got another sack full of it.

ALAN: It's good. What did you say it's called?

LENORE: French Lace. It came from Colbert's. Real expensive. Police are all over the place. The little ladies that live at the club come down the elevator, see all those uniforms, and go right back up to their rooms. Trish quit—her father's idea. She has been questioned, and he has too. We hear a lot of rumors but not many facts. They found Mr. Slocum's keys down in the back of the cushions on the sofa. Bruce says they weren't there when Mr. Slocum was killed. Everyone knows the two murders are related. Two murders! I can't believe I work in a building that has had two murders. Why did you call it "all that stuff"? If you don't want me to bring these things, just tell me.

ALAN: Do you see Ramona or Mrs. Slocum?

LENORE: Not a sign of Mrs. Slocum, but Ramona is in every day. Why? Which one of them do you think did it?

ALAN: I don't think anything about it. I've never seen any of them. All I know is what you tell me or what I read in the papers.

LENORE: That's what my brother used to call vegetables.

ALAN: What?

LENORE: "All that stuff." "Ahhhh, Mom, I don't want to eat all that stuff." Mother would say, "Those are beets, Roger. Say, 'I don't want to eat all those beets.' If you are going to be rude, be specific."

ALAN: I didn't know you had a brother.

LENORE: One. I have one.

ALAN: You never mention him.

LENORE: You never mention your family. I know you live with your brother in Englewood, but that's all I know.

ALAN: Well, I have one brother.

LENORE: That's all I've got. We're not very close. I'm closer to my sisters.

ALAN: Where does he live? Wisconsin?

LENORE: No. Upstate New York. Corning. He's in marketing.

ALAN: Do you get to see him?

LENORE: No. Like I said, we're not close. He left his wife and then married again. It was quite a shock to the family. I disapprove of that kind of thing.

ALAN: Divorce?

LENORE: Yeah, but the lifestyle more than the divorce. He said this new wife was the love of his life. His first wife, Beth, was a friend of mine. It was awful. I don't see why anyone would do that.

ALAN: What?

LENORE: Get involved like that.

ALAN: You mean, he had an affair.

LENORE: Yes. You sound so medieval. Roger said he couldn't help it. He loved this girl. Grandfather tried to talk to him once. We were all together on the back porch when Roger told us what had happened and that he and Beth were getting a divorce. Poor Beth. Everybody in town knew about it but her.

ALAN: What did your grandfather say?

LENORE: He said, "You fall in love from an accident of the heart. You love someone from a choice of the will. Roger, you've made a commitment to love Beth." It didn't do any good. Do you want more coffee? Candy?

ALAN: No. I want to put all this away.

LENORE: Why?

ALAN: I want to talk to you.

LENORE: That's what's the matter. We've got things to say. Last week, I was so disappointed when you weren't here. I really was.

ALAN: I told you I was . . .

LENORE: I know. It's all right. But it made me realize what it has meant to me seeing you each Friday. Fridays have been living places. Every place else has become unreal. When I go to work, I'm so used to being scared I no longer expect anything but fear. Little things have become ominous and threatening. My stamp box was overturned, and I wouldn't sit at my desk until the police checked it. I stood there and looked at the stamps and shook like I had a fever. Bruce brought me some coffee, and I began to cry—over nothing. Even Ramona . . .

ALAN: What about Ramona?

LENORE: Nothing. She's different to me. I wonder what she knows that she's not telling us. We know she and Mr. Slocum had a thing going. They met at a little French restaurant on 55th and Lexington. That's where she went when she left early or they had dinner brought in when he "worked late." I know Mrs. Slocum knew it. I know it, but she couldn't do anything about it . . . unless she . . . She is too frail, too fragile to kill someone. Ramona is tall and very together, in an artificial way. She came to my desk this morning. I was sitting with my head in my hands willing it to be five o'clock. She touched me like she would comfort me, but didn't know how. "We must bear up, all of us, until all this is over. We must be friends together. They cannot turn us against each other if we are friends." I cringed when she touched me. She saw it. "I have done nothing wrong," she said. "I, too, am a victim." It was very sad, but I couldn't feel sorry for her. She could have done it. Everyone who might be a friend could have done it.

ALAN: You mustn't be the judge and jury. Protect yourself. Don't take any chances. But don't convict everyone. It's better to have one murderer than 20 suspects.

LENORE: Janice thinks both these murders were for money. "Look for the secretary who is suddenly rich. She's there. Look for the secretary who has a new car. There'll be signs. You'll see." Janice is the kind of person who knows everything. She may be right about this. I don't know any of the secretaries very well. It's like I was telling you—I don't have anyone to talk to that's close. Janice is gone most of the time, and when we're together, she's always working on me. To improve me, she says. It was fun at first, being made over by someone who knew fashion and makeup. "The shoes must match the hem of your skirt. Not those shoes anyway. Those are only comfortable. Be comfortable when no one is watching. Outline the lid in violet and blend the rouge. You're not a clown, you're a beautiful young lady." Then it stopped being fun. It wasn't the makeup that was wrong. It was me—a girl from Fond-du-Lac who thought pâté wasn't half so good as goose liver with mustard and didn't understand why her shoes had to match her hemline. And all the borrowed clothes became uncomfortable because they weren't really mine. I've got a mother. I want a friend.

ALAN: You're just feeling the strain of those murders.

LENORE: No. It started before the murder of Mr. Slocum. I didn't have a place to enjoy me except here. That's why I came to New York. I didn't even "belong" in Fond-du-Lac, not after my brother had . . . well, Beth had been a good friend. After the divorce, I felt that Roger had betrayed his marriage and me. I wasn't enjoying the way everybody was living. I don't like going to bars or cocktail parties where you're supposed to "meet people." I don't enjoy drinking, and I think drugs are horrible. I tried to be a "swinger" there, and I hated it. I came here and tried to join in with the "set" I was meeting, but I couldn't. They don't talk . . . or listen. I wondered if I were out of my time. Maybe I got switched from the Victorian era. Don't laugh. It's possible. I could be in the crack of a time warp, and everybody like me is dead except for you.

ALAN: No, Lenore, a lot of us are like you. We all seek answers and make choices and become conformed to them.

LENORE: And your choice is Christ. That's what you're going to say. Well, mine isn't.

ALAN: I wasn't going to say that. You're the one who keeps mentioning Him.

LENORE: You think Him into what we're saying.

ALAN: I don't follow you. I'm a Christian, Lenore. To accept me, you've got to accept that. I may be a lousy Christian, I may be a hurting Christian, but I'm a Christian. I can't deny that just to make you feel comfortable. You can't be at ease with me and at odds with Him.

LENORE: Then what about Mac? What about Beth? What about Bangladesh?

ALAN: Lady, I don't have the vaguest notion what we're talking about. Who is Mac?

LENORE: The doorman who was killed. How did that happen?

ALAN: I don't know. Do you?

LENORE: No, but that proves your religion doesn't work.

ALAN: Why? Because I don't have answers?

LENORE: Yeah. No answers!

ALAN: Poor lady. For you, birds don't fly. You don't have that answer.

LENORE: But I'm not a bird. I'm a human being. I don't want a God who won't keep me safe from killings and broken vows and people who belittle me. *(Pause as ALAN stares at her)* Don't try to stare me down. I'm a logical person, and your religion isn't logical. Maybe I don't belong here, but I thought I did. Maybe I belong with the office parties and the bars and the world's great good times. I don't like the parties with the drinks and the gropers and the grabbers. I'm scared when I'm with them. It's not smart to drive when you're high or when you're drunk, and I hear them brag about it the next morning, how drunk they were and what near misses they had driving home. Someone could be killed. I don't even like it on television when cars are screeching around and it's supposed to be funny. I don't see people laughing at accidents. When they're hurt, they cry. When they hurt someone else, they . . .

(ALAN has moved away from her, in deep pain, and is standing by the rail facing out.)

LENORE: Alan? What's the matter? I'm sorry. Do you want some more chocolate?

ALAN: My son was killed by a drunken driver. A bunch of young people, they were good kids, but they were drunk. Their car went out of control turning a corner and slammed into my car. My boy was thrown out—killed instantly.

LENORE: Were you driving?

ALAN: No. I wasn't in the car, I was at my office. My wife was on her way to pick me up. We were going out of town for the weekend. My wife stopped the car to run into a drugstore to buy a new lipstick. She heard the crash. One of the girls in the other car was badly hurt but lived. The rest were OK. A few cuts. The driver had a broken ankle.

LENORE: Oh, Alan. I'm so sorry. When did it happen?

ALAN: Two years ago, but all of a sudden, it seems like yesterday. *(Struggling to regain composure)* After the accident, everything in my life fell apart. My wife and I had this horrible thing between us. She blamed herself for parking too close to the corner and wanting a new lipstick to match a new scarf. I blamed myself for having her pick me up when I knew her schedule was tight. All we shared was pain. We couldn't even grieve together. I lost my job. My brother heard about this opportunity, and I came by myself to try it for a year.

LENORE: Are you divorced, Alan?

ALAN: No, we wanted to get back together. I never knew how until now. You've shown me. That's what I wanted to tell you. To tell you and to thank you.

LENORE: Do you love her? Alan, look at me. You owe me that. Do you love her?

ALAN *(turning and smiling at her):* Yes, I do. I fell in love with her and married her and settled down to a good life in a good neighborhood with a good job, a good family, and a God who would keep me safe from killings and broken vows and—what else did you say?

LENORE: I don't remember. But God didn't deliver.

ALAN: My God didn't kill my boy. A car did, driven by a drunken driver.

LENORE: Your God allowed that?

ALAN: Yes, and that's hard. I don't understand it, but for me, birds fly. God would have grieved with me if I'd let Him. Somehow in all of this, there is God's love. He showed it clearly when *His* Son died. He shouldn't have to prove it again.

LENORE: I am sorry, very sorry. You should have told me.

ALAN: I know. That was wrong of me, but I felt I needed this place and our time together because you didn't know. There was nothing in your eyes or in your kindness to remind me. You didn't know the broken parts of me, and so with you, I let them heal. I began to feel again, to sense myself as a man. I heard the sound of laughter and was surprised to find it was mine. And yes, because of you, I was stirred again by romance and was glad it was not dead.

LENORE: Then there was love?

ALAN: Yes, oh yes. You are very lovable. But try to understand. This is not life. This is a cove, a haven, a forgotten corner of a garden. It's not life. Life is out there. What we found here has no structure.

LENORE: That's not true. You don't know that. Maybe we found something here so wonderful it will work out there.

ALAN: Like your brother did?

LENORE: That's not fair!

ALAN: Maybe it's not fair, but it is a logical reference.

LENORE: No, it's not! We're not like that. It's different in our case. Oh, that's not fair! I won't look at it like that. They were wrong. We are right. This has been good. I can't let it go!

ALAN: But you can't build a life on it. Our times have been episodes, repeated episodes, with no structure.

LENORE: And what gives structure if not repetition?

ALAN: Repetition doesn't give structure. It may not even give continuity.

LENORE: Then what does?

ALAN: Commitment! Structured commitment, an act of the will and not a whim of the heart. Not episodes held together by cashews and coffee and coincidence. When Anne and I met, we discovered what you and I discovered here. We enjoyed each other. We paid attention when we talked. Telling her about my day was more important than the day I lived without her. It was romantic and wonderful and alive. And in it, during it, and because of it, we considered that wonderful romance significant. We made a choice, a promise to take what we had discovered in our garden and maintain it out there in the world. I'm talking about the will to love, and I love Anne!

LENORE: You feel you are obliged to love her. That's not love. No woman would want that.

ALAN: No woman should have to settle for that, certainly not Anne. But the promise to love held me until I knew I loved her. I'm going to get her back. You taught me how. I can take her soup and crackers like your grandfather did. I can clear away the garbage every day. Together, Anne and I can share the reasonableness of grief because we are reasonable people, and by the grace of God, we can break through the hedge and find our garden still there. I can give her that. I can, I know it. Every woman loves a garden.

LENORE (very briskly): Well, thanks for the scenic tour. (Sounding quite a bit like Janice) I will not see you again, not here and not there. I'm sorry for the hurts you've had. I'm sorry that you lost your son, but I can't stay to comfort you. I feel cheated, tricked, and very embarrassed. (Definitely in tone like Janice) You can finish the fancy candy. I'll take my magic calliope, my umbrella, and my memories. You can keep the tray. Explain that to Anne. It might liven up a dull evening in your structure.

ALAN: Oh, Lenore. Don't stay with that act. It will only hurt more.

LENORE: That's not your problem. Good-bye. Incidentally, I can't stand the smell of cashews.

(Lights)

Scene 4

(ALAN *is seated, reading his newspaper.* LENORE *enters hurriedly.*)

LENORE: Alan.

ALAN: Lenore! And it's not even Friday.

LENORE: I'm sorry. I need your help. They found a tape in the secretary's office. It was the last letter Mr. Slocum dictated the night he was killed. At the end of it, as though he were starting another letter, he says my name.

ALAN: A letter to you?

LENORE: No, but as though he looked up and saw me in the outer office. He says, "Lenore . . . I didn't know you were working late." And then he laughs, and the machine is turned off. I didn't do it. I wasn't even there. I was here with you, but no one knows we've been meeting. Please help me. You're my only alibi.

ALAN: Was I here when you came the day of the murder?

LENORE: Yes. You were taking the garbage to 93rd Street. Remember? It was the day you gave me the music box.

ALAN: What about Janice?

LENORE: She picked me up later.

ALAN: Didn't she call you here?

LENORE: I gave her this number, but I could have called her from anywhere and still gotten here in time for her to pick me up. Will you help me?

ALAN: Yes, of course.

(Lights)

Scene 5

(ALAN *is at the bench with a newspaper. The telephone rings.* ALAN *lets it ring a few times and then answers it.*)

43

ALAN: Hello. *(Pause)* I think you have the wrong number. This is a public telephone in Riverside Park . . . Who? Yes. I know Lenore Barber, but she's not here. I don't expect to see her . . . hello? Hello. Hmmm. That's strange.

(ALAN hangs up the telephone and goes back to the bench. He looks behind the bench, retrieves the tin of cashews, opens it, finds a few crumbs, eats them with relish, and settles back to his newspaper as LENORE enters wearing the rainbow raincoat.)

LENORE: Hi. It's me. I just have a minute. Janice let me off at the corner. I told her I wanted to see you to thank you.

ALAN: Did you bring any cashews?

LENORE *(laughing)*: No. I know it was asking a lot of you—making us go public, but I really needed you. Can I write a note to your wife clearing you with her?

ALAN: No. She understands. I told her all about "us." She'll be here next week. We're going to find an apartment.

LENORE: Maybe you can have ours. Janice wants to move. She may go to Atlanta. She's found a buyer for the house in Tarreytown. This will be our last weekend there. I'm glad. I don't like going there anymore. I'm going to look for another job. They haven't solved anything over at the Hartley. Did you know they found the gun?

ALAN: Yeah. I read it in the paper.

LENORE: It was turned in to the lost and found from a taxi. The same gun killed both men. They traced the gun. It was Mr. Slocum's. Now the feeling is that Mrs. Slocum killed her husband. She said she was shopping, but no one saw her. She said, "I wasn't shopping to buy. I was only shopping to look, so no clerk waited on me." We can't imagine why she would kill Mac. Anything else I can clean up for you?

ALAN: You said once that a strange thing happened at the club. I keep wondering about it. What was it?

LENORE: A lot of strange things have happened. I don't remember what I was talking about.

ALAN: It had something to do with Mac. It was before the first murder.

LENORE: Oh yes. That was the private eye. Mac said someone in the club was being watched. He knew the investigator that was lurking around the building, followed Ramona one night when she left the office. It must not have been anything. Maybe someone who lives there was being watched, and they latched onto Ramona instead. I forgot about it when everything else happened.

ALAN: I'm going to miss all those people—the ones you bring with you.

LENORE: What people?

ALAN: The ones you've brought here. You do them well. I know each one. The little coffee girl, Ramona, Mrs. Slocum, Janice, your mother, your grandfather . . . I learned a lot from him. "You can outlive your dreams." I never see that inspector, the one you call Bruce.

LENORE: Bruce Presley. I guess I don't "do" him. Well, I better meet Janice. I do thank you. Bye. Oh, could you hand me that umbrella? It's Janice's. See? It matches. I want to give it back to her.

(ALAN *hands* LENORE *the umbrella from behind the bench.*)

LENORE: Don't be shocked. My hemline doesn't match my shoes. Bye. *(Exits)*

(ALAN *sits and picks up his newspaper. He slowly lowers the paper as a thought occupies him.*)

ALAN: Oh no! Lenore! Wait!

(ALAN *runs to the ramp, but* LENORE *is gone. He runs to the telephone, inserts coins, and dials.*)

ALAN: Get me the police. Yeah. This is an emergency. Could I speak to Inspector Presley? Bruce Presley. He's working on the Hartley Club murders. Please hurry! I know who the murderer is.

(Lights)

Scene 6

(ALAN *is sitting at the bench working on papers from his briefcase. The telephone rings. He lets it ring three times before answering it.*)

ALAN: Hello. *(Pause)* You have called a public phone in Riverside Park . . . What? No, this isn't a television repair shop. It's a public phone. You have the wrong number. *(Pause)* No, lady. I don't have your television. Look. You have the wrong number. Hang up and dial again.

(LENORE *enters from down right.*)

LENORE: Hi. I wondered if you'd be here today.

ALAN: Yes. This is my last day. We move into our apartment Sunday.

LENORE: How is . . . everything?

ALAN: Pretty good. We've got a long way to go, but we're getting there.

LENORE: I hear prayer helps.

ALAN: We're doing a lot of that.

LENORE: I'm thinking of trying it myself. It's very unsettling to know your room-mate is a murderer.

ALAN: I was sorry about Janice. I really was.

LENORE: I was too. I went by to see her. She tried to explain everything to me. Have you ever visited anyone in jail? Well, it's very strange. I sat there talking to her through that little mesh wall and still couldn't believe I was talking to someone who had killed two men. She and Mr. Slocum had been having an affair for years. She met him when he hired people through the employment agency where she worked. They were very discreet. She figured he was getting interested in another woman when he spent fewer weeknights at her apartment. He said he was spending more time at home, but she had him followed. That's when Ramona was being watched. Janice used me to keep her posted on the office. I never suspected it. The day she killed him, she was wearing the raincoat she had given me. Actually, it was one he had sent her. He had seen me that morning in it. That's why he thought it was me coming into his office.

ALAN: But you were wearing the coat that morning.

LENORE: But I left it at the apartment when I went home for lunch. That was the day that I made you the chicken salad sandwich. Remember? Janice came by the apartment to get the gun that he had given her for protection and picked up the coat because it was raining that afternoon. She wasn't planning to implicate me. That just happened.

ALAN: She went to Mr. Slocum's office to kill him?

LENORE: I don't think so—just threaten him. She was angry because she had just gotten the report from the man she hired to follow Mr. Slocum.

ALAN: How did she get past the security? Nobody knew her to let her in.

LENORE: One person did. Mac, the doorman, did. But he didn't see her come in. She entered the building in all the commotion about that big wedding, waited on the third floor until everyone was gone, and then walked into Mr. Slocum's office. He was finishing some dictating, looked up, and thought he saw me. Then he realized it was Janice and laughed. That's when he turned off the Dicta-phone, dropped off the dictation for the secretaries, and went back to calm down Janice. Janice said he was very smooth, very sure of himself. Janice told him to give up Ramona or she would tell Mrs. Slocum about their affair. He laughed and said Mrs. Slocum already knew and he had no intention of giving up Ramona. That was when she shot him. Once she knew he was dead, she did all the smart things to cover up. She called me from his office just like she was calling from the showroom. She had on gloves—no fingerprints.

ALAN: Surely there was something that connected her with Mr. Slocum.

46

LENORE: No. They had been very discreet. He gave her cash kept in a lockbox they had in a Yonkers' bank. It was a lot of money. It'll pay for a lawyer. That's why she took his keys. She thought that his key to their lockbox was on that ring. When she found it wasn't, she came back to look for it in his office. It was the only thing that could have involved her.

ALAN: Did she find it?

LENORE: No. It had been found, and the police were checking on it. While she was looking for it in the office, Mac found her. She felt she had to kill him since he recognized her.

ALAN: How? The raincoat?

LENORE: No, but that raincoat is why Mac thought I was involved in Mr. Slocum's murder. He caught a glimpse of Janice leaving the building after she had killed Mr. Slocum.

ALAN: And that's why he wanted you to have lunch with him. Wait a minute. You said Mac recognized her.

LENORE: Uh-huh. She had gotten him the job as doorman. He and I were the only possible links between her and the Hartley Club . . . and the key. You know, she doesn't feel any remorse about killing Mr. Slocum, but she does about Mac. It was so awkward talking to her. At first, she acted as though everything were normal and we were meeting for coffee or over her desk. She made small talk about clothes and asked me to bring her makeup. Then she said, "Why did Mac come into the office? He ruined everything." I'm going to send her makeup to her. I don't think I'll go myself to see her again.

ALAN: Where are you living now? Did you keep the apartment?

LENORE: Heavens, no! I didn't stay there another night. The police stopped us on the way to Tarreytown. Thank you. You may have saved my life. You're a hero—a real one. I don't know what to say. Thank you seems small for my life. The police pulled us over, and Janice thought she'd been speeding. Then they asked for my driver's license and had me get out of the car, and *then* they arrested Janice. I couldn't believe what was happening. A policeman drove me back to the city. I didn't want to go back to the house or the apartment, so I . . . I . . . called my brother. Well, I guess we've wrapped up the mysteries. We were walking through the park, and I wondered if you were here. You said I brought a lot of people into this corner—all but Bruce. So I thought I'd show you Bruce.

ALAN: Good. One last character to finish the cast.

(ALAN *sits to watch* LENORE.)

LENORE: No. I mean the real Bruce. I don't know how important he is to the rest of my life, but he's a friend, and I'd like you to meet him. *(Calling off right)* Bruce. Bruce. Come here. I want you to meet Alan.

(Curtain)

PERFORMANCE LICENSING AGREEMENT

Lillenas Publishing Resources
Performance Licensing
P.O. Box 419527, Kansas City, MO 64141

Name _____

Organization _____

Address _____

City _____ State _____ ZIP _____

Play title _____ ***INTERVAL*** by Jeannette Clift George _____

Number of performances intended _____

Approximate dates _____

Amount remitted* $ _____

Mail to Lillenas at the address above.

Order performance copies of this script from your local bookstore or directly from the publisher 1-800-877-0700.

*$30.00 for EACH performance. Payable U.S. funds.

PERFORMANCE LICENSING AGREEMENT

Lillenas Publishing Resources
Performance Licensing
P.O. Box 419527, Kansas City, MO 64141

Name _____

Organization _____

Address _____

City _____ State _____ ZIP_____

Play title _____*INTERVAL* by Jeannette Clift George_____

Number of performances intended _____

Approximate dates _____

Amount remitted* $_____

Mail to Lillenas at the address above.

Order performance copies of this script from your local bookstore or directly from the publisher 1-800-877-0700.

*$30.00 for EACH performance. Payable U.S. funds.